Toulouse-Lautrec: Paris Album

Henri de Toulouse-Lautrec

PARIS ALBUM

With an introduction & descriptive notes
by David Piper

London
The Folio Society
1958

Printed in Great Britain by
The Haycock Press Ltd, London
Set in 11 point Garamond 2 point leaded
Bound by Dorstel Press Ltd, Harlow

Introduction

Toulouse-Lautrec is so small he makes me dizzy.—Mme Tristan Bernard.

On November 24, 1864, at Albi in the south of France, was born Henri-Marie-Raymond de Toulouse-Lautrec-Monfa. His stock was one of the oldest and noblest in France, but in him it freaked; he had a congenital weakness of the legs, offset by what was to prove an abnormal strength of visual perception. From his childhood onwards, he drew voraciously, and especially after 1878, when he broke a leg for the first time. The next year he broke the other leg, and soon it was clear that his legs were never to grow normally. He set for life into a crippled mis-shape, with a normal body and dwarf-sized legs.

His physical deformity was surely a decisive factor in his resolve to become a professional artist (a career unheard-of in his family). He studied to begin with under two artists of orthodox practice and theory in Paris, first with the academic and fashionable portrait painter, Bonnat, and then with Cormon (where he met, especially, Vincent van Gogh). In 1885 he established his own studio at No. 7 Rue Tourlaque, and there he worked for some thirteen years—almost the entire compass of his brief maturity. His life and his work centred mostly in and around Montmartre, and both living and working were driven at a pitch that would have killed many far stronger men more quickly than it did him; pencil in hand, he haunted music-halls, cafés, bars, brothels, circuses and theatres; the stimulants that kept him going were drink, women, and his work. In 1889, he first showed at the Salon des Indépendants; in 1891, his revolutionary work as a poster-artist began, and in the year after, his first colour-prints. Production during the next few years was intense until, in 1898, his health began to betray grave signs of strain. By 1899, his addiction to drink had become a morbid alcoholism, and, after a complete breakdown, he had to withdraw to a private asylum at Neuilly, where he stayed for three months. Recovering for a spell, he emerged, only to succumb finally and fatally. He died on September 9th, 1901, in his thirty-seventh year.

The major artistic influences on his work were two: Degas, and the Japanese masters of the colour-print. In his earliest lithographs he tended to use colour and mass much as a painter does, but soon he developed a technique, light and swift as a bird's flight, of drawing on the stone that was unsurpassed by any earlier lithographer, and which tells especially in his monochrome prints; hardly any artist has rivalled him in the art of omission. But his dominant instinct was always for the raw material, for life itself, and for life manifest in individual men and women. He saw them clearest—and in passion if not in kindness—in their moments of heightened emotion; hence his craving for all places where life is keyed up by drama and sport, by sex and by drink. In endless show, men and women revolved before him, and the limelight of his eye fell on them, sharpening as hunger. It is in this essentially human approach of his work that he stands apart from his artist-contemporaries, the first great generation of the Post-Impressionists—Gauguin, Seurat, Vuillard, Bonnard; only Van Gogh perhaps has the same devotion to people, though from an entirely different angle. It is almost easier to compare Lautrec with the great realist writers, with Zola and de Maupassant, than with the artists; his account of human sexual display, especially, sometimes parallels theirs, and was revolutionary in the visual arts.

And the stage on which he saw his compulsive creatures was *par excellence* Paris, and particularly, the quarter of Montmartre—that Montmartre evoked by Léon Daudet: 'A Paris within Paris, a city apart, infinitely strange, full of contrasts, of shadows and gloom, of flashes of bright light . . .' Most of Lautrec's best lithographs are set in Paris, and it is to his unique, still-living, vision of Paris in the 'nineties, especially of the city after dark, that fantastic teeming civilization of midnight, that this selection of them is devoted.

Lautrec, the winged gnome, grows greater with each day that passes. . . . He was among the most inventive artists of the late nineteenth century—and of all time.— Claude Roger-Marx.

D.P.

Contents

1. *Au Moulin Rouge: la Goulue et sa Sœur*

The famous dance-hall, the Moulin Rouge, opened in Montmartre in 1889, and began to overshadow its chief rival, the Elysée-Montmartre, when it enticed thence a famous troupe of dancers. The leading star was one *La Goulue* (born Louise Wéber) who ravished Lautrec's eye to the exclusion of many—until it caught on Jane Avril. La Goulue's speciality was the *quadrille naturaliste*, a development of the by now old-fashioned can-can, the girl kicking high and over her partner's head. From a superb torso, La Goulue kicked higher, faster and with more brio than anyone else. Yvette Guilbert, in her memoirs, described her dancing—'in black silk stockings, with one foot clad in black satin held in her outstretched hand, she swirled the sixty yards of lace on her petticoats till the drawers showed, with a heart coquettishly embroidered plumb central on her little seat. . . . She sent her partner's hat flying with a neat and tidy kick, and sank into a split, her body erect, her waist slim in sky-blue satin, her black satin skirt spread about her like an umbrella five yards in circumference.'

But her triumph was short; by 1893 already, the greed that had won her her nickname was loading her with fat, and two years later she had sunk to a travelling sideshow on fair-grounds. Thence her decline, hastened by drink, was inevitable; she died in 1929, a charity patient at the Lariboisière hospital. In character she was never charming, notorious for her gross appetite, foul-mouthed, vindictively jealous. The woman shown with her here was a colleague at the Moulin Rouge, known as *la môme Fromage*, an eccentric woman whose strong claim to be La Goulue's lover was as strongly denied by La Goulue, who said she was her sister. In the background is the Anglo-Australian painter Charles Conder, who was for some time much with Lautrec about Montmartre.

This print, already astonishingly assured, was in fact Lautrec's first attempt in lithography.

1892

2. L'Anglais au Moulin Rouge

The cult of a certain Englishness in masculine clothes and fashion was fairly widespread in Paris in the 'nineties; English tailors and English tea-shops flourished in the Rue St. Honoré and in the Rue de Rivoli, while an English hatter in the Boulevard Haussman advertised his address without any compromise as 'Haussman Street'. Lautrec too subscribed to this anglophile urge, and various Englishmen were for a time his frequent companions, notably the painter, Conder, and the poet Arthur Symons. Here, the male profile, with its assured, satisfied moustache, and the stance, the clothes—the faultless hat, the high choker collar and the smartly proportioned cravat, the gloves, the cane—encompass an image of the ideal of a certain sort of mashing, dandaisical Englishness: the lady-killer, the Anglo-Saxon about Montmartre. The identity of the Englishman has been something of a mystery; he had been said to be a Mr Warner and to have been some kind of theatrical agent, but he has now been shown to be one Mr W. T. Warrener of Lincoln.

1893

3. Jane Avril

Illegitimate daughter of an Italian nobleman and a Parisian *demi-mondaine*, Jane Avril was born in 1868; her childhood was tormented by appalling cruelty and neglect, and ended in a nervous breakdown. When she was seventeen years old she ran away, and, after four years of odd jobs, arrived at the Moulin Rouge as a dancer in 1890. At first overshadowed by La Goulue in the eyes of the public in general and of Lautrec in particular, about 1893 she began to hold the artist's attention as had La Goulue before her, and he drew her again and again. In marked contrast to the blatant if splendid vulgarity of La Goulue, Jane Avril's leg movements seem to have been sideways rather than upwards, almost refined in gesture. Many writers as well as artists sensed in her a *fin-de-siècle* aura, and the poet Arthur Symons (a friend of Lautrec's) wrote of her 'morbid, vague, ambiguous grace', of her mysterious smile:

> *A shadow smiling*
> *Back to a shadow in the night . . .*

Lautrec scarcely saw her thus. Whether she approved of his vision of her, or not, is obscure; but years later, in her reminiscences, she acknowledged gratefully that in fact she owed her fame to him—'It began after he had made his first poster of me' (for her performance at the Jardin de Paris in June, 1893). They got on well together; she was a girl of some intellectual yearnings, a reader of books, and at home in studios—according to one account, not especially impressed by Lautrec's talent, but 'revelling in the smell of paint as other women dote on music or on flowers'. Later, she became a music-hall star of international reputation.

From Le Café-Concert, *1893*

4. *Aristide Bruant*

A large man of sinister flamboyance, Aristide Bruant tried his hand at many trades until, in 1885, at the age of 34, he started a cabaret in Montmartre—Le Mirliton. He wrote (in meticulous *argot*), composed, and sang his own songs; their subject-matter was drawn from the miseries and vices of the very poor, of which he had intimate knowledge, assiduously maintained. In action, he howled his ballads 'with his hands in his pockets, occasionally getting across the sensation of genius by sheer enthusiasm'. He capitalized on his romantic profile, accented by a lock of jet-black hair, by framing it between a large black sombrero and a voluminous cape-like jacket with a sanguinary red scarf. He used to woo and win his audiences by insulting them—once he greeted the arrival of Lautrec and two companions with a shout of—*Hush, gentlemen! here's that great artist Toulouse-Lautrec with a friend of his—and a pimp that I don't know!* By 1892, Bruant was famous, and in demand at the most fashionable of Parisian cafés-concert, including Les Ambassadeurs, where he is shown here. By 1895, he had made enough money to retire handsomely to a country life; he made few reappearances until 1924, when at the age of 73 he scored a last, resounding success at the Empire music-hall. He died in 1925.

His appearance in Montmartre more-or-less coincided with that of Lautrec, who was very intimate with him up to about 1894. Some of Lautrec's best-known posters are those of Bruant, and he made many illustrations for his songs—ruthlessly stark interpretations of their themes, shedding Bruant's essentially vulgar and sentimental emotion as a jagged rock sheds the ebbing tide; this study, of one who was one of the artist's closest companions, is equally ruthless.

From Le Café-Concert, *1893*

5. La Modiste

One of the rare almost 'sweet' lithographs by Lautrec—in spite of the hat, venomous as a scorpion, with which his model is skirmishing. (The box at her side, as fantastic in size as is the hat in shape, is typical of the period; the magnificent idiocy of the hats then in fashion demanded containers even more ostentatiously and luxuriously expendable; such boxes were not included in the price of the hat, but had their own separate reckoning—*extra*.)

This drawing is inspired by Degas (his *Les Modistes* of 1882, for example); Lautrec was a close neighbour and fervent admirer of his. Degas was not only interested in the same sort of subject-matter as Lautrec—notably circus, horses, dancers—but his technique of draughtsmanship and cold clarity of vision remained a decisive influence on Lautrec throughout the younger artist's mature work. The occasion for this study was a dinner at the Salon des Indépendants—the annual exhibition originally sparked off in revolt against the academic Salon, and the arena in which many of the great Impressionist and Post-Impressionist painters, including Lautrec, showed their work.

The model is believed to be Renée Vert, who had a small shop in the Faubourg Montmartre. Lautrec first knew her when she was living with Adolphe Albert, a fellow-student of his at the studio of Fernand Cormon, about 1883. She is also said to have been Lautrec's mistress for some time.

For the menu at the Salon des Indépendants 23 June 1893

6. *Leloir et Moréno dans 'Les Femmes Savantes'*

A scene from Act III of Molière's evergreen satire on pedants and the blue-stockings who dote on them, *Les Femmes Savantes*, first performed in 1672. On the left Trissotin, the affected wit, is declaiming an absurdly precious sonnet, *For the Princess Urania, upon her Fever*, to his assembled feminine followers, ranged rapt on the right. Trissotin in this performance was played by Louis Leloir; the actress immediately on his right, in profile, is the then-famous Marguerite Moréno—both of them staple actors in the classic tradition of the Comédie Française. In 1903, Moréno was to resign from this company on the grounds that no one cared any longer for poetry, and that she no longer had the chance to play the great classic parts.

September 1893

7. *Une Redoute au Moulin Rouge*

A gala-night at the Moulin Rouge was a fairly frequent occasion, on which processions in elaborate fancy-dress were staged, the mounts being supplied by the famous donkeys of Montmartre, one of the tourist sights. The rider of one of the donkeys is again La Goulue, whom Conder desired so much. ('They say she is bad and dances nude at the Café Americain after 12 o'clock —I myself have been prone to admire her in a spiritual sense, money always restraining the physical.') The fame of the Moulin Rouge had flared very fast, and all through the 'nineties it was an irresistible draw (though later it gave way to some extent to the Folies-Bergère) for both British and American tourists, generally male. 'You could see there', wrote one contemporary, 'many English tourists, over for three days, wearing knickerbockers and golfing-caps, and smoking little pipes.' But by 1900 it was a necessary port-of-call for the more determined sight-seers of both sexes, and in that year the *Guide des Plaisirs à Paris* indicated (for the information of indigenous sight-seers) amongst the objects worthy of attention at the Moulin Rouge, a few visiting 'English families, with a dozen children . . . scandalized by the sight of these women who dance with one another . . . whose muscular elasticity, when their legs open wide in the *grand écart*, indicates a corresponding elasticity in their morals. And when the lace petticoats of the dancers suddenly surge waist-high, in a far-too-suggestive swirl, prudish Albion veils her face and beats a hasty retreat.'

1893

8. Le Coiffeur

Designed for the programme of the play *Une Faillite* by Björnstjerne Björnson (1832–1910). This great Norwegian was a dynamic figure in both literary and political spheres throughout his long life; though he is overshadowed now, outside his own country, by his contemporary and compatriot, Ibsen, he made a major contribution to the development of the realist drama in Europe. *En Fallit* ('A Bankruptcy') was one of the first of his plays in this manner, 'the earliest raising of the veil upon Norwegian domestic life'. The actor-manager Antoine, who produced the French version of the play (the first staging of any Björnson play in Paris) at the Théâtre-Libre, considered that it was 'the most pathetic tragedy about money that had ever been put on the stage'. But neither the public nor the critics agreed with him. Sarcey, most influential of critics, wrote—quite unfairly, for Björnson's play had been produced originally in Norway twenty years earlier—that this was a *comédie de genre* modelled on the French pattern, 'and less well done than are all those plays of which it is reminiscent: *a quoi bon alors!*' Antoine, whose financial affairs were going from bad to worse at the time, could appreciate the irony of the title only too well.

Programme for Une Faillite, *at the Théâtre-Libre, November 1893*

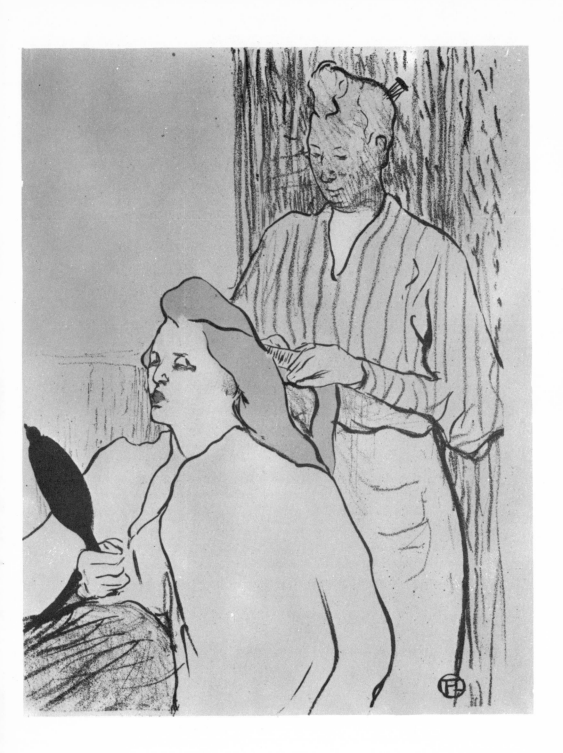

9. Au Moulin Rouge: Un Rude! Un Vrai Rude!

The melancholy, sunken man on the right, in profile with the nutcracker nose and chin, is the landscape painter Joseph Albert, a friend of Lautrec's from his student days on. The bearded figure in the foreground, with the wolfish snap of teeth—*le rude! le vrai rude!*—is Lautrec's father, the Count Alfonse de Toulouse-Lautrec-Monfa. The Count is here unusually and perhaps maliciously sited, for his normal hunting-grounds were certainly not dance-halls. Although his son once said of him that he 'only went gay on café-au-lait', his eccentricities were as remarkable as those of Lautrec, but in a different sphere. Descendant of the great house of Toulouse, that once ruled over half of France, he had that kind of feudal panache that does not fit easily into modern society. An athlete, an arrogant dandy, a fine horseman, his energy tended to dissipate itself in freak activities, not only in the normal hunting-field but in the chase of otters through the streets of Paris, dressed as a Canadian trapper; in milking his Cossack-saddled mare in the Bois de Boulogne when thirsty; in wearing a kilt for dinner, washing his linen in the gutters of the Place de la Madeleine and hunting rats with a revolver.

Although profoundly disillusioned by the physical deformity of the last of his line, his son and heir, and though he never admitted that an aristocrat of Toulouse blood could properly be a professional artist, he recognized and was grateful for his son's achievement even if he never understood it. He refused to interfere in Lautrec's way of life (unlike one of the family who ostentatiously burned some of his pictures), and once said, in defence of the cripple, that the family should be grateful to him for not cursing them for having born him into the world as he was. Lautrec, on his side, inherited from his father that passionate delight in sport, in all physical movement whether of humans or of animals, that burns in so many of his drawings. The epithet *un rude* is probably used here ambivalently—both in its literal sense, and also, flatteringly, with reference to the work of the famous sculptor, François Rude.

Published in L'Escarmouche, *10 December 1893*

10. *Sarah Bernhardt dans 'Phèdre'*

Sarah Bernhardt's revival of Racine's *Phèdre* opened on November 19, 1893, at the Renaissance-Théâtre, which she had bought as actor-manager in March of that year. For a French tragic actress, the part of Phèdre is the final test of greatness, as that of Hamlet is for an English actor; Bernhardt was then in her fiftieth year, but incomparably the greatest actress in France, and her performance in this revival was acclaimed as one of her finest. The critic Sarcey wrote: 'It's strange, astounding, inexplicable, but nevertheless true, that Bernhardt is younger, more splendid, and—let's face it—more beautiful than she has ever been: of a more artistic beauty, which gives one a shock of admiration as does the sight of a beautiful statue.' Arthur Symons, remembering her in the light of this lithograph, conveys more of the *frisson* of the 'nineties—'terrific—she, a shadow of guilt made mercenary by lust of forbidden love, and furious by her anguished sense of unachieved desire. Lucien Guitry is one huge black heap, such as one imagines in that oppressive heat when August twilight merges into night; he is not even the mockery of a malignant shade: but, as one struck suddenly with an intense horror of her, his blood surges into his cheeks. And she, this perverse Jewess, poses, wide-eyed; her eloquent lips seem about to utter Racine's frenzied lines . . .'

Drawn for L'Escarmouche, *24 December 1893*

11. *Ida Heath au Bar*

A meditation upon two of Lautrec's favourite *motifs*: bars, and English music-hall dancers (to Ida Heath in action on the boards he devoted a separate lithograph—see No. 21). A brilliant piece of characterization, this drawing, with its floating melting curves stabilized by the sober verticals of the spruce barman behind and the downward dagger-thrust of the upside-down bottle, evokes very vividly the agreeable, slightly muzzy, slightly spiced, interchange of conversation lubricated by alcohol.

1894

12. *La Loge au Mascaron Doré*

This magnificently dramatic design (with the dissolute profile of Charles Conder on the left of the box) was for the programme-cover for *Le Mission-aire*, which opened at the Théâtre-Libre in 1894. At this theatre, since 1887, the great actor-manager Antoine had been producing experimental plays, offering 'a haven for young writers and a laboratory for experiment', and exerting a profound influence on contemporary French theatre. 'Antoine', wrote the critic of *Le Temps*, 'has performed the service of bringing us back to exact observation of the milieu', and the forte of the Théâtre-Libre lay in a kind of social realism, inspired by the practice and example of such masters as Zola and Ibsen, and by a distaste for outworn conventions of acting. The play for which Lautrec made this programme design was however a more stylized affair, described by Antoine as a 'story in five tableaux, interspersed with commentaries by a reader'; the reader, 'at the side of the stage, acting as a classical chorus, commented on and presented each episode one after the other'. For some reason, this formula exasperated the wrath of the public beyond bounds; the preceding year had anyway been a very poor one for almost all the theatres, owing to the increasingly popular competition from the music-halls, and when one night Antoine himself (playing the reader) had a handful of *sous* thrown in his face, he took the hint and abandoned the struggle for the time being, departing on a European tour.

Programme for The Missionary, *by Marcel Luguet, at the Théâtre-Libre,* 24 *April 1894.*

13. *Réjane et Galipaux dans 'Madame Sans-Gêne'*

Réjane (properly Gabrielle-Charlotte Réju, 1856–1920), one of the most celebrated French actresses of her time, enjoyed a long career of the most distinguished variety of accomplishment; in 1905, she acquired the Nouveau-Théâtre, which became the Théâtre-Réjane. Here Lautrec has drawn her in a famous dancing-lesson scene from Sardou's play *Madame Sans-Gêne*, revived at the Vaudeville in 1894. This is a costume-piece, centred on the life of the wife of Lefebvre, one of Napoleon's marshals—the part played by Réjane herself. The play itself was described as not much of a play—rather 'a series of *tableaux-vivants*', and the production remarkable mainly as a sumptuously furnished and dressed spectacle of the Napoleonic era—and for Réjane's performance. One critic complained that the appeal was too much to the eye alone: a complaint that Lautrec would surely not have endorsed.

1894

14. Cissy Loftus

Here shown as a mimic of male singers, Cissy Loftus was eighteen years old when Lautrec drew her. She became a great favourite at Les Décadents, one of the cafés-concert that the artist frequented a great deal, in the Rue Fontaine. It seems to have lived up to its name—opening in 1893, forcibly closed by the censor in 1894, re-opening in 1895. It specialized in British stars, including the English dancer May Milton and the Irish singer May Belfort. Cissy Loftus was a born mimic, who 'seemed to work from the inside of her subjects outwards'; born in Glasgow, she made her debut at the age of seventeen at the Oxford Music Hall shortly after leaving the Convent of the Sacred Child at Blackpool. Her appearance in Paris was brief; in England and America her long and distinguished career continued a little uncertainly between the rival claims of the music-halls, operetta and the 'straight' theatre; latterly she spent most of her time in the United States, and it was in New York that she died, in July 1943.

1894

15. *La Goulue Danse avec Valentin-le-Désossé*

For an account of La Goulue (Louise Wéber), the leading female dancer at the Moulin Rouge in the early 'nineties, see No. 1. Valentin-le-Désossé, Boneless Valentine, was her starring partner in the quadrille. He had danced with her at the Elysée-Montmartre, and moved with her to the Moulin Rouge. His real name was Jacques Renaudin, and he was, by day, manager of a small café near the Halles Centrales, emerging at night into his rôle as perhaps the best-known male-dancer in Paris. He was a performer, as his nickname indicates, of astonishing double-jointed agility, 'so thin that you could wrap him round a gas-pipe'; he appeared always in the same invariable clothes—like 'nothing so much as a dissolute undertaker on a spree'—in an aged black frock-coat, a tall silk hat well forward over the beak-like nose that projected in complement to the thrusting bony jaw. He is said to have been strictly an amateur, never taking money for dancing; yet of the two of them—La Goulue and himself—Valentin was the most professionally creative, inventing new steps and teaching them to his partner. He was devoted, but apparently platonically, to her; he used to go fishing with her, and to advise her on the cultivation of her garden, and was often to be seen driving her out ceremonially in his carriage in the Bois de Boulogne.

1894

16. La Tige (Moulin Rouge)

One of the most sinister of Lautrec's intimations of depravity; the girl, La Tige, whom the swollen-faced man seems to be accosting, was one of the many dancers at the Moulin Rouge, distinguishable most easily perhaps one from the other when they kicked high and their names, writ large on the soles of their dancing-shoes, advertised for a flashing second their identities. Images such as this seem almost to justify what might otherwise have been thought a somewhat over-sensitive appreciation of the spectacle of the Moulin Rouge at night, made by an American visitor in 1895: 'It glows like a furnace, and the glare from its lamps reddens the sky and lights up the surrounding streets and cafés and the faces of the people passing like a conflagration. The mill is red, the thatched roof is red, the arms are picked out in electric lights in red globes, and arches of red lamp-shades rise on every side against the blackness of the night. Young men and women are fed into the blazing doors of the mill nightly, and the great arms, as they turn unceasingly and noisily in a fiery circle through the air, seem to tell of the wheels within that are grinding out the life and the health and souls of these young people of Montmartre.'

1894

17. Miss May Belfort

An Irish girl, May Belfort appeared at Les Décadents in 1895, in an act which rapidly became famous. She came on stage dressed as an infant in a voluminous yellowish nightgown, her black hair tumbling from under a vast white night-bonnet. The glimpse of black cradled in her arms is a kitten; she stood perfectly still, using no gestures, and sang in a babyish voice in English:

> *I've got a little cat*
> *I'm very fond of that . . .*

Her innocence was denied only by an occasional flash of bold black eyes and by the notoriousness of her far-from-private life; she was also one of the few regular feminine habituées of the Irish and American Bar, where Lautrec was almost always to be found at this period at the hour of the *apéritif*. Like others before her, May Belfort seems to have obsessed his eye, and he made many drawings and lithographs of her until his interest in her was exhausted.

1895

18. Mlle Marcelle Lender en Buste

Marcelle Lender, the famous actress, had attracted Lautrec's attention several times in the early 'nineties, but her performance in Hervé's *Chilpéric* at the Variétés in 1895 seems to have hypnotized him. In this operetta she produced brilliant versions of Spanish dances like the bolero and the fandango, and Romain Coolus complained that he was dragged some twenty times by Lautrec to see her performance—'She was dressed, or rather undressed, in such a way that not a single muscle of her back escaped the scrutiny of the levelled opera-glasses. When, after the sixth time, I got a bit tired of hearing the famous chorus, I asked Lautrec why he insisted on glutting me night after night with such trite tunes. 'I come only to see Lender's back,' he answered. 'Look at it carefully; you will seldom see anything so magnificent. Lender's back is splendid. . . .' But Lautrec in fact studied her from all angles, made innumerable drawings, and one of his finest paintings represents her in action in the bolero. The actress's reactions to Lautrec's view of her were typical of those that he usually provoked in his female subjects. 'He's very fond of me,' she said. 'But as far as portraits are concerned, you can keep him.'

1895

19. *Procès Arton—Déposition Ribot*

Between 1890 and 1895, a series of scandals, that shook the government of France, followed one upon the other, following the investigation of the failure of a French company in a canal-project in Panama. Some very famous people were involved, notably Ferdinand de Lesseps (the builder of Suez) and his son, and the brilliant engineer Eiffel. One of the key middlemen involved in charges of widespread bribery in the highest quarters was Léopold-Emile Aron (better known as Arton), a broker born in Strasbourg in 1850. He avoided arrest by levanting from France, but was tried by default and sentenced. Run to earth in London in 1895, he was extradited and brought to trial in person. After proceedings of extraordinary and somewhat dubious complexity, he was in the end acquitted; he remained however a suspect person, and committed suicide in 1905. The trial monopolized the attention of the Parisian public when in progress in 1896; it seemed as though a far bigger cause than Arton's was on trial, perhaps even that of the Government of France itself.

Lautrec, unlike Daumier and Forain, was not generally fascinated by the spectacle of the law in action, but he did attend several sessions of this particular trial and made many drawings on the spot, though from them he designed only three lithographs of which this is one. Ribot, here seen giving witness, had a long political career. He became a minister (Foreign Affairs) in 1890, and, in January 1895, Président du Conseil briefly until October, when he fell. Later he often held office, notably as Minister of Finance between 1914 and 1917.

1896

20. *Irish and American Bar, Rue Royale*

The Irish and American Bar, near the Madeleine, was No. 33 Rue Royale, next door to Weber's (which in the end absorbed it). The manager in Lautrec's day was an Englishman, and the bar sported a celebrated barman, Ralph, who claimed to be a half-breed of Chinese and Red Indian blood. The bar had a fairly exotic and varied clientèle: English jockeys, the coachmen of the high aristocracy, literary and theatre people, circus performers—Footit the clown used to go there—and, from about 1895 on, very often Lautrec. In the heart of Paris it retained something of the flavour of an English pub, and it seems to have baffled a French journalist who wrote it up for *La Vie Parisienne* in 1896: 'An English bar, full of proper soaks seated in silence opposite the barman and lost in contemplation of rows of bottles; on the walls hang sporting prints, and the single note of gaiety in the whole establishment is provided by the red of the jockeys' coats. . . .' The barman, Ralph, is shown here in action with a cocktail shaker, while the portly drinker is one of Lautrec's favourite subjects—'You see that stout man at the bar?' said Lautrec to Gauzi: 'The one wearing a top-hat, the one wearing a flower so elegantly in his button-hole? He's the Rothschilds' coachman—isn't he *marvellous*?'

Poster, for The Chapbook, *1896*

21. Ida Heath, Danseuse Anglaise

Ida Heath would be all but forgotten by now, were it not for the fact that Lautrec saw her, was intrigued, and devoted two of his best lithographs to her (see No. 11). Inevitably, the scene here recalls Degas, but Degas would never have permitted the individual irony, the demonic smirk, that informs this brilliant portrait. Ida Heath, technically a 'transformation dancer', was well-known in the 'nineties both in Paris and in London, where she performed at music-halls like the Tivoli alongside Robey, Albert Chevalier, Little Tich and Dan Leno. Colette, in a series of music-hall stories, written much later but surely relevant, left some vivid sketches of typical English stage-girls abroad —there was one she called Glory: 'As she is blonde and young, thinnish, with blue eyes, she answers to all that we expect to find in a *petite danseuse anglaise*. She speaks a little French, her voice as thrusting as a duckling's, and she puts such a useless effort into pronouncing a few words of our language that it makes her cheeks flush and her eyes shine. . . . She is not as pretty as Daisy, that devilish brunette, always either in tears or in a fury, dancing like a demon or taking refuge up the stairs, whence she spits abominable English expressions . . . or the sultry Edith, who exaggerates her accent deliberately to make you laugh, and proffers, ingenuously, in French, enormities of the meaning of which she is perfectly well aware. . . .'

1896

22. Conquête de Passage

In 1892, Lautrec was asked to decorate the *salon* of a brothel in the Rue
d'Amboise (the main feature of the decorations was a series of medallions
featuring portrait-heads of the inmates), and from then until about 1896 he
drew on brothel-life extensively for the subject-matter of many of his most
famous paintings. He would, for weeks at a time, settle in at one of these
maisons-closes, announce its address as his address, and carry on his day-to-day
business from it. The prim and elderly Durand-Ruel, the famous art-dealer,
once made an appointment with Lautrec at an address in the Rue des Moulins,
and was reduced almost to collapse to find himself in a brothel being introduced to the girls.

Lautrec used to talk to Yvette Guilbert about his life in these establish-
ments, and two remarks of his, recorded by her, indicate the roots of its
fascination for him. The reaction of the physical oddity who could never
hope to attract a normal physical response—'Ah *love*! you can sing about love
in any key you like, Yvette, but hold your nose, dear, hold your nose! If you
were to sing about *desire* one might understand, might even be amused at the
variousness of those rushes of blood, but love! my poor Yvette, *love* does not
exist.' And yet, in contrast to this, the almost surgically austere creed of the
artist: 'Always and everywhere, ugliness has its accents of beauty—the thrill
is to reveal them where no one else notices them. . . .' In the astringent
embrace of his line, he revealed the women of the brothels as they were, yet
without salaciousness, in a curiously becalmed, almost domestic, tranquillity.

From Elles, *an album of ten lithographs published by Gustave Pellet, May 1896*

23. Clownesse Assise

The sitter (or squatter) in Pierrette costume is Cha-U-Kao, Chinese or at least of Chinese pseudonym, a model who served Lautrec on several occasions. Her main haunts seem to have been the Moulin Rouge and the Nouveau-Cirque in the Rue Saint-Honoré, which was—if not the most popular—certainly the most fashionable of the many similar shows in Paris—the circus of the *gens-du-monde*. The 'nineties, in spite of the booming competition from the music-halls, was the golden age of circus, and performances went on throughout the year (the cinema, ultimately to prove one of the main factors in its decline, was then embryonic). Lautrec never lost his delight in the spectacle of the ring, in acrobats, trick riders and clowns, and it was on the circus that he concentrated, during his collapse and internment in 1899, when he produced a remarkable series of drawings on circus-themes, accurate to the last detail and extraordinarily vivid and alive—all done from memory.

From Elles, *1896*

24. Au Bar Picton

The Bar Picton, at No. 4 Rue Scribe, was one of several bars in the neighbour-hood of the Madeleine patronized by Lautrec; it was run by Achille Picton ('generally referred to by men about town simply by his Christian name'), who enchanted Lautrec by always addressing him as 'Monsieur le Vicomte Marquis'. On the far side of the window-glass the words 'American Bar' are clearly legible, which has led to some doubts that it is Picton's bar that is really the subject here; but whichever bar it is, it indicates the direction of Lautrec's taste at this period. He was a pioneer in France of that American speciality, the cocktail, and Gauzi has left us an account of the artist's own private activities as a barman, priest of the cult, compounding a cocktail (a 'rainbow', the recipe borrowed from one of these bars: curaçao, anisette, picon, lemon-juice and angostura, served iced with a zest of lemon dusted with sugar). For one party, besides wearing the traditional white coat, Lautrec went so far as to shave off his beard and moustache, the better to play the part.

1896

25. *La Grande Loge*

For Lautrec, the theatre and the music-hall always offered a double spectacle, a play within a play: the audience and the decoration of the theatre as much as the actors, the stage itself and its décor. His eyes were opened no doubt to this cross-cut angle of vision by Degas, as also were those of Sickert, who was recording the Old Bedford and other London theatres and music-halls at much the same time as Lautrec was busy in Paris. (Sickert incidentally considered Lautrec a poor artist, probably because the Englishman thought of Lautrec too much in terms of Degas to be able to see his true originality.) Lautrec went to theatrical performances with a sketch-book; his pencil was seldom idle and he missed little—the whole business entranced him. As Paul Leclercq wrote: 'He loved the atmosphere of the theatre, its peculiar smell, the elegant manners of the attendants who checked the tickets, the broad gangways, the foyer, the green-room. . . .'

One of the women seated in the first box is said to be Mme Brazier; the solid, solitary phlegmatic of immense distinction, in the top-hat, in the third box, is Tom, the Rothschilds' coachman, a favourite model of Lautrec's (see No. 20). According to Yvette Guilbert, the coachmen of the great used to hold converse of considerable pomp amongst themselves, addressing one another in cafés by the titles of their masters; 'Eh, d'Uzes, how about a throw of *zanzibar*? De Luynes will hold my horses; I've just won ten *sous* off that *miteux* of a d'Larochefoucault. . . .' The lithograph itself shows most clearly the profound influence of the Japanese masters of the colour-print upon Lautrec, and it is also one of his finest achievements in any medium, more successful even, in its reduction to absolute essentials, than the oil-painting he made of the same subject.

January 1897

26. L'Automobiliste

About 1896, motor-cars, in the weird and wonderful shapes of early experiment, began to attract the attention of the cartoonists, and so too did their
drivers, capped and goggled, in protective clothing as exotic to the eye of the
'nineties as space-men to the eye of the nineteen-fifties. A typical motor-car is
described in *La Vie Parisienne* of this year: 'An *up-to-date* model, a machine
with the strength of innumerable horses, and with such feather-lightness,
such sweetness of steering—it's a dream! Enormous tyres on all wheels;
panels beautifully picked out in colour, the cushions *dernier cri* in English
leather. Unfortunately though, all this does not prevent that sempiternal din
of loose ironmongery that persuades passing bicyclists that their own chain
has come off, nor that vague yet penetrating odour of grease and oil, nor, one
must admit, the fact that the *ensemble* is profoundly unaesthetic in appearance.
The servant, perched in the rear, in full livery like the guard of a coach, seems
here completely miscast—a mechanic in blue overalls would be far more
suitable.'

The driver portrayed here is Lautrec's cousin and constant companion,
Tapié de Céleyran. A doctor, he introduced Lautrec to the Hôpital International, where the painter made some extraordinary studies. He was a
bizarre contrast to the dwarfish Lautrec, tall and gangling, a very old-
seeming young man: 'His black pomaded hair was parted at the back of his
head and brushed carefully over his temples; between his high cheekbones,
and flanked by a pair of side-whiskers (clipped in the Austrian fashion to
leave the chin bare), an enormous, red and pimply nose crowned by gold-
rimmed spectacles stuck out as if emerging from a piece of fur; his antiquated
clothes looked like garments lifted from an old family portrait. . . .'

1896

27. *A La Souris*

La Souris was the best-known Lesbian café in Paris, in the Rue Breda. Abnormalities always fascinated Lautrec, himself trapped inescapably in the abnormality of his crippled body. A friend who went with him to La Souris, Paul de Lapparent, described him seated under the harsh light of electric lamps, 'enthroned, surrounded by a dozen women flabby in flesh and dressed in tight-fitting men's jackets and stiff collars'. For a time he seems even to have taken up residence there, as he had done earlier in the *maisons closes*; he was accepted by the regulars and known as 'M. Henry'. The woman in this drawing is the proprietress of the establishment, Madame Palmyre, whom Paul Leclercq remembered as 'a buxom woman with the ferocious appearance of a bulldog, who, though in reality remarkably kind-hearted, always seemed to be on the point of biting'. The character of her dog, the real bull-dog, the famous Bouboule, was more in keeping with its appearance; it was notorious for its antagonism against the female clients of La Souris, and on the slightest suspicion of friendly advances from them, would drench their ankles under the table. Lautrec made also a lithograph of Bouboule for a menu for a dinner at La Souris the same year.

June 1897

28. *La Danse au Moulin Rouge (Les Deux Amies)*

Unusual amongst Lautrec's lithographs, as it is based directly on a painting that he had made of the same subject previously (now in Budapest). The dancers, judging by the severe masculine cut of their clothes, are presumably Lesbians; one of them is the *clownesse* Cha-U-Kao, who worked mainly at the Noûveau-Cirque and at the Moulin Rouge, and of whom Lautrec made other studies. The feminine figure on the right, with her back towards the spectator, is in sharp contrast with its flouncing bustle and frivolous coat—she is the dancer, Jane Avril. In the background, sitting at tables beyond the balustrade, two of Lautrec's constant companions are recognizable. On the extreme right is the clean-shaven, fair-headed painter, Charles Conder; on the extreme left, with the top-hat and the sharp, dark beard, the artist François Gauzi. The latter was an old friend of Lautrec's since their student days in the early 'eighties, and he left a revealing account of him: 'At Cormon's atelier, Lautrec made a great effort to copy the model exactly; but in spite of himself he exaggerated certain typical details, sometimes the general character, so that he distorted without trying to or even wanting to. I have seen him force himself to prettify his study of a model; in my opinion without success. The expression *se forcer à faire joli* is his own.'

July 1897

29. Girl Selling Fish

The subject is of a kind that is fairly rare in Lautrec's lithographs: an every-
day street scene. It is part of a design for a book-cover; while he produced of
course various picture-books, these were, to describe them more strictly,
series of lithographs with almost incidental texts, if any (like the famous
Yvette Guilbert series) rather than book-illustrations. In 1898 he made a
remarkable set of lithographs for G. Clemenceau's *Au Pied de Sinai*, which
dealt with life in the ghettos of Poland but for the material of which Lautrec
drew on Jewish slums in the Tournelle quarter of Paris. He also made studies
of animals for Jules Renard's *Histoires Naturelles*, 1899, and began but never
finished illustrations for the famous realist novel by de Goncourt, *La Fille
Elisa*. Besides these, he designed a few book-covers, of which this is one.

Detail, from the cover for Les Courtes Joies, *a book of poems by J. Sermet, 1897*

30. L'Amazone et le Chien

One of several lithographs featuring horses that Lautrec made towards the end of his life; Madame Hansman, a horse-dealer, has been suggested as the rider. At this date, the horse had far from lost its battle with the emergent automobile, and the great diurnal social display in Paris took place on horseback or in a horse-drawn carriage in the Bois de Boulogne, as in London it did in Rotten Row. Though Lautrec has here isolated his sitter—as elegantly dark and elegantly sinister as any of Constantin Guys' characters—men and women usually went to the Bois to see and to be seen, and 'when all these people meet in the afternoon on their way to and from the Bois, there is no better entertainment of the sort in the world, and the Avenue des Champs-Elysées grows much too short. . . . There are women in light, billowy outfits, with elbows squared and whip in hand, fearlessly driving great English horses from the top of a mail-phaeton . . . narrow-chested, corseted and padded young Frenchmen in white kid gloves, who hold one rein in each hand as little girls hold a skipping rope . . . fat Hebrew bankers and their equally fat dogs in open Victorias. . . . If you look from the Arc de Triomphe to the Tuileries you see a broken mass of glittering carriage-tops and lace parasols, and what looks like the flashing of thousands of mirrors as the setting sun strikes on the glass of the lamps and windows and on the lacquered harness and polished mountings. . . .'

1897

31. Yvette Guilbert sur la Scène

After a childhood harsh with poverty, but redeemed by a mother of extra-ordinary courage and probity, Yvette Guilbert worked her way through jobs as model, counterhand, and dressmaker, to her first important engagement at the Moulin Rouge in 1890. But she really made her name at the Divan Japonais, a café-concert in the Rue des Martyrs, so minute that the intimate atmosphere so necessary for her art was almost inevitable. Indeed the reason behind her failure at first to catch on with the public lay in the very originality of her act; she was the first of the great *diseuses*, and by 1892 was famous in Paris as the first to 'achieve the art of making obscenities palatable by putting them across nonchalantly and in a drawling monotone, which enables her to sing the most outrageous songs with an illusion of innocence'. She made few concessions, and she was not beautiful—too thin, too long in the neck: as *La Vie Parisienne* wrote in 1894—'Her hair is too yellow, her lips too red, her gloves too black, her sash too green—but she is a great artist', and the hold of the weak voice and of the precisely careless languor of the thin body over the audience was absolute.

Lautrec, like most people, was fascinated by Yvette Guilbert, but he made her a greater return than anyone else; her art was ephemeral but she lives in his portraits. At first repelled, she grew to be almost fond of him, but although she accepted his versions of her, she did not welcome them. One of his earliest attempts—a sketch for a poster—was returned by her: 'For the love of heaven, don't make me so astoundingly ugly!'—and his first series of lithographs of her, though she agreed to sign them, left her *estomaquée*; most of her friends thought them revolting, and some urged her to take legal action against Lautrec. In fact, both series show the artist at the peak of his form as a lithographer; rarely has so formidable, vital and haunting an image been achieved with such a minimum of means.

Lautrec drew two series of lithographs of Yvette Guilbert; the frontispiece to the present volume is from the first of them, 16 lithographs published as the Album d'Yvette Guilbert, *Paris, 1894. This plate is from the second, known as the English Series, published in London in 1898.*

32. *Au Hanneton*

Le Hanneton, at No. 75, Rue Pigalle, was presided over by a formidable *patronne*, Mme Armande; it was one of the most popular cafés in Lesbian circles, and, like La Souris (see No. 27), much frequented by Lautrec especially between 1897 and 1898, the years when he was most fascinated by this particular perversion. They were also the years in which a marked deterioration, both physical and mental, became very evident in Lautrec, preceding his breakdown; his search for stimulation and for subject-matter through all the *bars, brasseries, estaminets, tavernes, cabarets, mastroquets, liquoristes, débits, bistros, grands cafés honnêtes et crapuleuses, petitites bistrailles* of Paris was undermining his health with imminent alcoholism, and also, to some extent, his work—though not in this case. Here the pictorial depth is managed, in the foreground, with all the old consummate and brilliant economy; the characterization of his splendidly dressed sitter stringently indicated in the contrast of her flouncing costume with the harsh mouth and the ravage of the eyes, and with the rodent-like little dog.

1898

33. Le Jockey

In 1899, the year of his breakdown and withdrawal into a private mental home, Lautrec began what was meant to be a volume of lithographs devoted to horse-racing—*Les Courses*. It was never completed, but this lithograph, made for it, is rightly one of his most famous works. Influenced by Degas, it yet conveys, as even Degas never did, the often strangely awkward yet immensely powerful union of speed and sheer massiveness in a racing horse. Lautrec's passion for horses (which, after the tragic final stunting of his legs in his late teens, he could never ride) dated from his early boyhood and owed much to the enthusiasm of that remarkable horseman, his father. His early sketch books are full of horse-studies, and though in early manhood his interest flagged, about 1895 it seems to have revived, and he went to many of the Paris meetings—here, no doubt as in his delight in all sports, sublimating his passion for movement and for speed.

Then as now, the race-meetings, especially at Longchamps, formed one of the chief focuses of the social season, and the Jockey Club was one of the most exclusive of Parisian clubs. At the heart of the race-meeting was *la tribune des femmes du monde*, whose feminine habituées were described by *La Vie Parisienne* in 1894—'Almost all of them dating from a good way back, but loyal to the customs of the good old days. Not dressed in the height of fashion, but they know the form—both of horses and of men. They talk a great deal, and very loud. . . . In the last few years, a few new ones come there, daughters of owners or of trainers. There are even some foreigners, English or American women. *Très sport*, this younger generation, and not shy of technical talk. . . .'

1899

34. Le Paddock

Another race-course scene, for Lautrec's never completed series—*Les Courses*. A contemporary account of typical goings-on in the paddocks of Parisian race-meetings suggests that not much has changed there at least: 'It's there that congregate the people (rare) who know the form, and the people (very numerous) who don't know the form. It's there that you can hear just about as many idiotic remarks as you can in front of a picture in the Louvre, and that you can see people, who don't know the difference between a bus-horse and a Shetland pony, lay down the last word on hindquarters or on heaviness in the shoulders.'

1899

35. Au Bois

'The Bois de Boulogne is compassionate towards those poor wretches who
sleep out in its shade, and agreeable to Parisian families who stroll there with
their infants—those hot-house blooms, so fine, so delicate, that the robust
babies of London seem open-air flowers in comparison. In the morning, as
the lawns wake milky under a light coverlet of dew, through the mist-veiled
trees comes the cavalcade of horsemen and horsewomen, carriages and smart
young women who come here to exercise the seduction of their smile and the
originality of their clothes. Then the Allée des Acacias is coloured with
shining umbrellas, and as loud with flirts as a fashionable casino. . . .' So
wrote a somewhat idyllic contemporary.

Lautrec leaves the age of the girl in the Bois uncertain; if her dress seems
almost infantile Kate Greenaway, he allows no hint of childish candour in her
face: she might almost be May Belfort out for a walk in full stage disguise.

1899

36. Le Marchand de Marrons

This study of the vendor of hot chestnuts, a typical street scene of the time, was Lautrec's last lithograph. After he came out in May 1899 from his brief sojourn in the mental hospital, he held off more or less successfully for some time his dipsomanic craving for alcohol; but, early in 1900, it proved too strong for him, and thereafter his decline, though irregular, was inevitable. He spent the winter of 1900 in Bordeaux, and in the spring came to Paris for the last time; he was working hard most of the time, with variable efficiency, though some of his work from this period is as good as ever. By July he was clearly dying, and withdrew to one of the family houses, the Château de Malrome. He painted on, being lifted on to a ladder to reach his work, until he had no longer strength enough. He died on September 9th, 1901, two months before his thirty-seventh birthday.

April 1901

Acknowledgements

Any student of Lautrec's lithographs must start with three works: firstly, L. Delteil's *Le Peintre Graveur Illustré*, vols. X and XI, 1920; and then M. Jean Adhémar's excellent catalogue of the exhibition at the Bibliothèque Nationale, *Œuvre Graphique de Toulouse-Lautrec*, 1951, and also the Catalogue of the Arts Council Exhibition, *Toulouse-Lautrec*, 1951. I am heavily indebted to these three publications.

The following works especially are of great assistance:

> Douglas Cooper, *Henri de Toulouse-Lautrec*, 1955
> F. Gauzi, *Lautrec et son Temps*, 1954
> G. Mack, *Toulouse-Lautrec*, 1938
> M. Joyant, *Henri de Toulouse-Lautrec*, 1927
> Yvette Guilbert, *La Chanson de ma Vie*, 1927

The passage from Colette's *L'Envers du Music-Hall* on number 21 is quoted by permission of the publishers, Messrs Martin Secker and Warburg, and three passages from Yvette Guilbert's *La Chanson de ma Vie* on numbers 1, 22, 25, by permission of Editions Bernard Grasset.